Maths
made easy

Key Stage 2
Ages 10–11
Advanced

Author John Kennedy
Consultant Sean McArdle

Certificate ☆ ☆ ☆ ⭐

Congratulations to ....
(write your name here)

for successfully finishing this book.

☆ *You're a star!* ☆

DK

D0537287

Cubes of small numbers

★

What is 2^3?

$2 \times 2 \times 2 = 8$

2 cm

What is the volume of this cube?

$2 \times 2 \times 2 = 8$ cm^3

You find the volume of a cube in the same way as working out the cube of a number.

Use extra paper here if you need to. What is...

3^3

4^3

6^3

5^3

1^3

2^3

What are the volumes of these cubes?

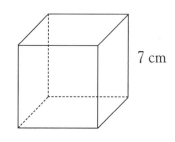

7 cm

cm^3

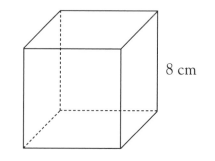

8 cm

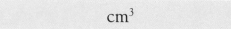
cm^3

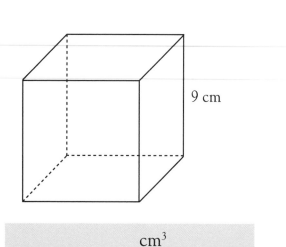

9 cm

cm^3

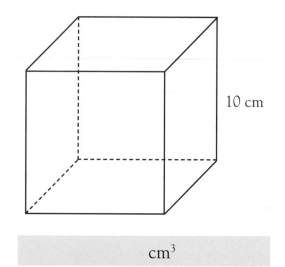

10 cm

cm^3

Cubes of larger numbers

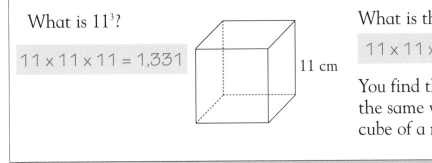

What is 11^3?

$11 \times 11 \times 11 = 1,331$

11 cm

What is the volume of this cube?

$11 \times 11 \times 11 = 1,331$ cm³

You find the volume of a cube in the same way as working out the cube of a number.

Use extra paper here if you need to. What is…

12^3 _____

20^3 _____

19^3 _____

25^3 _____

15^3 _____

13^3 _____

50^3 _____

100^3 _____

What are the volumes of these cubes?

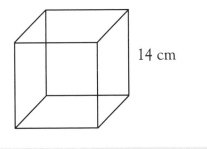

14 cm

_____ cm³

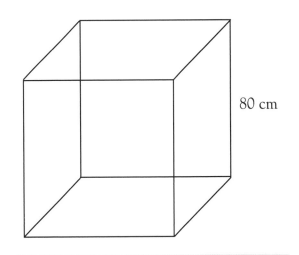

80 cm

_____ cm³

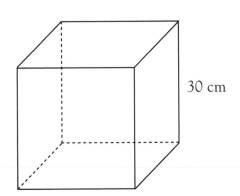

30 cm

_____ cm³

13 cm

_____ cm³

3

Fraction problems

Find $\dfrac{3}{5}$ of £30.00.

£30.00 ÷ 5 = £6.00 ($\frac{1}{5}$)

£6.00 × 3 = £18.00 ($\frac{3}{5}$)

$\frac{3}{5}$ of £30 is £18

Find $\dfrac{7}{10}$ of 60 cm.

60 cm ÷ 10 = 6 cm ($\frac{1}{10}$)

6 cm × 7 = 42 cm ($\frac{7}{10}$)

$\frac{7}{10}$ of 60 cm is 42 cm

Find $\dfrac{3}{5}$ of these amounts.

40 cm

£50

£10.50

80 m

75 g

45 kg

Find $\dfrac{7}{10}$ of these amounts.

48 m

£98.00

75 km

Find $\dfrac{2}{3}$ of these amounts.

48 cm

120 kg

£24.00

Finding percentages

Find 30% of 140.

(Divide by 100 to find 1% and then multiply by 30 to find 30%.) $\frac{140}{100} \times 30 = 42$

Find 12% of 75. $\frac{75^3}{100_{\cancel{4}_1}} \times \cancel{12}^3 = 9$

Find 30% of these numbers.

620   240

80   160

Find 60% of these numbers.

60   100

160   580

Find 45% of these amounts.

80 g   40 cm

240 ml   600 km

Find 12% of these amounts.

£150   £600

125 m   775 m

★ Factors, multiples, and prime numbers

Write all the factors of these numbers.

12	1, 2, 3, 4, 6, 12	18	1, 2, 3, 6, 9, 18
25	1, 5, 25	64	1, 2, 4, 8, 16, 32, 64
72	1, 2, 3, 4, 6, 8, 9, 12, 18, 24, 36, 72	96	1, 2, 3, 4, 6, 8, 12, 16, 24, 32, 48, 96

What are the common factors of these numbers?

15 and 25

72 and 108

48 and 64

150 and 125

Circle the multiples of these numbers.

Multiples of 3	9	15	26	54	62
Multiples of 5	17	25	43	70	95
Multiples of 8	26	32	56	62	96

Write the first three common multiples of these numbers.

3 and 5

4 and 7

Write the prime numbers between these numbers.

1 and 20

20 and 50

Add and subtract fractions

☆

Work out these sums.

$$\frac{1}{4} + \frac{5}{6} = \frac{3}{12} + \frac{10}{12} = \frac{13}{12} = 1\frac{1}{12}$$

$$\frac{7}{9} - \frac{2}{3} = \frac{7}{9} - \frac{6}{9} = \frac{1}{9}$$

Remember: Use equivalent fractions to make the denominators the same.

Add these fractions. Give answers as improper fractions if necessary.

$\frac{1}{3} + \frac{1}{3} =$ ☐ $\frac{4}{11} + \frac{3}{4} =$ ☐ $\frac{6}{9} + \frac{12}{18} =$ ☐ $\frac{3}{5} + \frac{4}{10} =$ ☐

$\frac{3}{8} + \frac{2}{8} =$ ☐ $\frac{1}{5} + \frac{3}{5} =$ ☐ $\frac{2}{5} + \frac{6}{15} =$ ☐ $\frac{4}{7} + \frac{2}{5} =$ ☐

$\frac{2}{6} + \frac{3}{12} =$ ☐ $\frac{5}{9} + \frac{3}{9} =$ ☐ $\frac{2}{7} + \frac{4}{7} =$ ☐ $\frac{2}{5} + \frac{3}{9} =$ ☐

$\frac{5}{8} + \frac{4}{12} =$ ☐ $\frac{1}{4} + \frac{3}{8} =$ ☐ $\frac{4}{10} + \frac{3}{10} =$ ☐

Add these mixed fractions. Give answers as mixed fractions.
Remember: First change them to improper fractions.

$1\frac{1}{4} + 3\frac{1}{4} =$ ☐ $3\frac{1}{3} + 4\frac{1}{2} =$ ☐ $2\frac{2}{5} + 2\frac{3}{5} =$ ☐

$2\frac{3}{4} + 1\frac{2}{3} =$ ☐ $1\frac{4}{5} + 3\frac{3}{10} =$ ☐ $4\frac{5}{8} + 2\frac{3}{4} =$ ☐

Subtract these fractions. Write answers in simplest form.

$\frac{3}{5} - \frac{2}{5} =$ ☐ $\frac{3}{4} - \frac{7}{12} =$ ☐ $\frac{3}{5} - \frac{1}{3} =$ ☐ $\frac{1}{3} - \frac{1}{4} =$ ☐

$\frac{4}{5} - \frac{7}{10} =$ ☐ $\frac{5}{8} - \frac{3}{8} =$ ☐ $\frac{11}{15} - \frac{2}{5} =$ ☐ $\frac{1}{2} - \frac{2}{7} =$ ☐

$\frac{2}{3} - \frac{4}{9} =$ ☐ $\frac{5}{6} - \frac{2}{3} =$ ☐ $\frac{7}{9} - \frac{2}{9} =$ ☐ $\frac{1}{2} - \frac{5}{12} =$ ☐

Subtract these mixed fractions. Give answers in simplest form.
Remember: First change them to improper fractions.

$4\frac{2}{5} - 3\frac{4}{5} =$ ☐ $2\frac{5}{8} - 1\frac{7}{8} =$ ☐ $5\frac{4}{9} - 4\frac{2}{9} =$ ☐

$2\frac{2}{3} - 1\frac{3}{4} =$ ☐ $2\frac{1}{2} - 2\frac{3}{8} =$ ☐ $4\frac{5}{6} - 3\frac{2}{3} =$ ☐

Multiply fractions

Work out these sums.

$$\frac{2}{3} \times \frac{1}{2} = \frac{2 \times 1}{3 \times 2} = \frac{2}{6} = \frac{1}{3}$$

$$\frac{2}{5} \times 2 = \frac{2}{5} \times \frac{2}{1} = \frac{2 \times 2}{5 \times 1} = \frac{4}{5}$$

Multiply these fractions. Give answers in their simplest form.

$\frac{3}{4} \times \frac{1}{2} =$ 　　　　　$\frac{3}{5} \times \frac{2}{3} =$

$\frac{3}{10} \times \frac{2}{5} =$ 　　　　　$\frac{1}{2} \times \frac{3}{7} =$

$\frac{2}{3} \times \frac{1}{4} =$ 　　　　　$\frac{5}{8} \times \frac{2}{4} =$

$\frac{7}{10} \times \frac{3}{4} =$ 　　　　　$\frac{1}{2} \times \frac{5}{8} =$

$\frac{2}{3} \times \frac{4}{10} =$ 　　　　　$\frac{3}{5} \times \frac{2}{6} =$

$\frac{4}{9} \times \frac{1}{3} =$ 　　　　　$\frac{2}{3} \times \frac{5}{6} =$

Multiply these fractions by whole numbers. Give answers as mixed fractions.

$\frac{2}{3} \times 4 =$ 　　　　　$\frac{3}{5} \times 2 =$

$\frac{3}{4} \times 6 =$ 　　　　　$\frac{3}{10} \times 5 =$

$\frac{5}{8} \times 3 =$ 　　　　　$\frac{4}{7} \times 8 =$

$\frac{1}{5} \times 9 =$ 　　　　　$\frac{1}{4} \times 4 =$

$\frac{5}{12} \times 3 =$ 　　　　　$\frac{6}{11} \times 2 =$

$\frac{5}{9} \times 3 =$ 　　　　　$\frac{10}{100} \times 4 =$

Divide fractions

Work out these sums.

$$\frac{1}{3} \div 2 = \frac{1}{3} \div \frac{2}{1} = \frac{1}{3} \times \frac{1}{2} = \frac{1}{6}$$

$$\frac{4}{7} \div \frac{3}{5} = \frac{4}{7} \times \frac{5}{3} = \frac{4 \times 5}{7 \times 3} = \frac{20}{21}$$

Divide these fractions by whole numbers. Give answers in their simplest form.

$\frac{1}{3} \div 3 \ =$ $\frac{4}{5} \div 2 \ =$

$\frac{3}{8} \div 2 \ =$ $\frac{1}{4} \div 6 \ =$

$\frac{1}{2} \div 5 \ =$ $\frac{3}{4} \div 7 \ =$

$\frac{7}{10} \div 3 \ =$ $\frac{2}{9} \div 5 \ =$

$\frac{3}{7} \div 3 \ =$ $\frac{2}{5} \div 4 \ =$

$\frac{2}{3} \div 6 \ =$ $\frac{5}{6} \div 3 \ =$

Divide these fractions. Give answers as a mixed number if needed.

$\frac{1}{2} \div \frac{1}{3} \ =$ $\frac{3}{4} \div \frac{2}{3} \ =$

$\frac{3}{5} \div \frac{1}{6} \ =$ $\frac{5}{7} \div \frac{2}{5} \ =$

$\frac{2}{9} \div \frac{3}{5} \ =$ $\frac{5}{8} \div \frac{1}{2} \ =$

$\frac{7}{10} \div \frac{1}{4} \ =$ $\frac{3}{7} \div \frac{4}{9} \ =$

$\frac{4}{5} \div \frac{5}{6} \ =$ $\frac{1}{4} \div \frac{3}{10} \ =$

$\frac{2}{5} \div \frac{1}{3} \ =$ $\frac{1}{8} \div \frac{9}{10} \ =$

Ratio and proportion

A rat has 7 babies every 4 months.
How many babies does the rat have in one year?

21

In a class, there are 2 girls for every 3 boys.
There are 10 girls. How many boys are there?

In a week, a dog eats 4 cans of dog food with 7 biscuits.
How many biscuits are needed for 24 cans?

A cook uses 6 apples with 300 g flour to make an apple
crumble. How many apples are needed with 1.5 kg
of flour?

In a bathroom, a black tile is used for every 5 white tiles.
How many black tiles are needed for 60 white tiles?

An account earns £2.50 interest for every £10,000 saved.
How much interest is earned on £150,000?

A rectangle is drawn with length 5 cm x width 8 cm.
If it is drawn 4 times larger with length 20 cm, what is
the width?

A model of a building uses the scale 10 cm = 200 ft.
The model of the building is 75 cm high. What is the
actual height going to be?

Algebra

Work out this equation.

$a + 5 = 7$	$10 - b = 4$	$a + 4 = 14 - 6$
$a + 5 (-5) = 7 (-5)$	$10 - b (+ b) = 4 (+ b)$	$a + 4 = 8$
$a = 2$	$10 (-4) = 4 + b (-4)$	$a + 4 (-4) = 8 (-4)$
	$b = 6$	$a = 4$

Find value of each letter.

$a + 6 = 24$ $b - 5 = 14$

$a + 28 = 42$ $b - 17 = 17$

$a + 17 = 25$ $b - 27 = 23$

$10 + y = 12$ $16 - x = 4$

$38 + y = 50$ $26 - x = 9$

$42 + y = 64$ $42 - x = 20$

Solve these equations.

$15 + a = 42 - 17$ $y + 13 = 7 \times 5$

$100 - b = 72 + 14$ $x - 42 = 96 \div 8$

$63 + a = 9 \times 9$ $21 - y = 40 - 25$

Write equations for these problems and then solve them.

Laura had a bookcase overloaded with books.
She gave 24 to a school fair. She had 36 left.
How many books did she have to begin with?

Dan collected comics. He was given a set
of 12 for his birthday. He now had 64 in his
collection. How many comics did he
have before his birthday?

More algebra

★

Work out this equation.

$10 - a = a$	$3b + 15 = 12 \times 6$	$27 \div c = 9$
$10 - a\,(+\,a) = a\,(+\,a)$	$3b + 15\,(-15) = 72\,(-15)$	$27 \div c\,(\times c) = 9\,(\times c)$
$10 = 2a$	$3b = 57$	$27 = 9c$
$10\,(\div\,2) = 2a\,(\div\,2)$	$3b\,(\div\,3) = 57\,(\div\,3)$	$27\,(\div\,9) = 9c\,(\div\,9)$
$a = 5$	$b = 19$	$c = 3$

Find value of each letter.

$5a = 25$

$a = 36 - a$

$6a = 42$

$3y + 8 = 20$

$6y - 16 = 38$

$42 - 5y = 22$

$15 \div c = 5$

$32 \div c = 8$

$56 \div c = 7$

$d \div 4 = 7$

$d \div 9 = 5$

$d \div 11 = 10$

Solve these equations.

$56 - a = 26 + 2a$

$2b + 16 = (12 \times 3) - 2$

$4y - 27 = 72 \div 8$

$48 \div d = 7 + 5$

$17 + c = 26 - 2c$

$4e + 45 = 35 + 6e$

Write equations for these problems and then solve them.

Isla bought two packets of biscuits and a 20 pence bunch of bananas. The total cost was 80 pence. How much is one pack of biscuits?

Jodie invited 48 guests to her New Year party. 10 people couldn't make it and half of the rest were going to arrive late. How many were going to be on time?

Multiplication by tens and units

Work out the answer to each sum.

```
   527          834
 x  76        x  58
 36,890       41,700
  3,162        6,672
 40,052       48,372
```

Work out the answer to each sum.

```
   426          895          632          778
 x  84        x  65        x  39        x  49
```

```
   597          994          632          747
 x  46        x  37        x  64        x  75
```

```
   428          147          236          145
 x  95        x  62        x  87        x  33
```

```
   346          529          485          763
 x  85        x  72        x  29        x  84
```

Multiplying decimals

Work out these sums.

1.456	1.456	1.456	1.456
x 10	x 20	x 3	x 23
14.56	29.12	4.368	29.120
			+4.368
			33.488

Multiply these numbers.

2.567	4.687	8.924	3.963
x 10	x 10	x 100	x 100

12.892	7.689	9.578	15.432
x 100	x 1,000	x 1,000	x 1,000

Multiply these numbers.

0.456	0.351	1.764	14.23
x 2	x 4	x 8	x 3

0.859	1.034	8.049	69.23
x 7	x 6	x 5	x 3

2.836	0.765	5.218	62.73
x 12	x 18	x 30	x 45

1.873	20.72	708.7	8.302
x 60	x 21	x 15	x 40

14

Division by units

47÷2 can be written in two ways:

$23\frac{1}{2}$ or 23.5

$2\overline{)47}$ $2\overline{)47.0}$

Write the answers to these sums with fraction remainders.

$2\overline{)17}$ $4\overline{)19}$ $3\overline{)16}$ $4\overline{)37}$

$3\overline{)29}$ $2\overline{)45}$ $5\overline{)87}$ $5\overline{)49}$

$4\overline{)73}$ $3\overline{)35}$ $4\overline{)93}$ $5\overline{)69}$

Write the answers to these sums with decimal remainders.

$2\overline{)73}$ $2\overline{)85}$ $2\overline{)39}$ $4\overline{)59}$

$4\overline{)71}$ $4\overline{)83}$ $5\overline{)29}$ $5\overline{)47}$

$5\overline{)24}$ $2\overline{)77}$ $4\overline{)38}$ $5\overline{)93}$

Write the answers to these sums choosing decimal or fraction remainders.

$2\overline{)37}$ $2\overline{)59}$ $4\overline{)93}$ $4\overline{)51}$

$5\overline{)21}$ $2\overline{)83}$ $4\overline{)31}$ $5\overline{)63}$

More division by units

94÷8 can be written in two ways:

$$11\frac{\cancel{9}^{\;3}}{\cancel{8}_{\;4}} = 11\frac{3}{4}$$

$8\overline{)9^{1}4}$

or

11.75

$8\overline{)9^{1}4.^{6}0^{4}0}$

Write the answers to these sums with fraction remainders.

$6\overline{)95}$ $\qquad$ $7\overline{)73}$ $\qquad$ $9\overline{)88}$ $\qquad$ $8\overline{)55}$

$7\overline{)51}$ $\qquad$ $9\overline{)85}$ $\qquad$ $6\overline{)73}$ $\qquad$ $7\overline{)65}$

$9\overline{)94}$ $\qquad$ $8\overline{)33}$ $\qquad$ $7\overline{)74}$ $\qquad$ $6\overline{)63}$

Write the answers to these sums with decimal remainders.

$6\overline{)39}$ $\qquad$ $8\overline{)68}$ $\qquad$ $5\overline{)62}$ $\qquad$ $8\overline{)34}$

$5\overline{)91}$ $\qquad$ $6\overline{)75}$ $\qquad$ $5\overline{)49}$ $\qquad$ $8\overline{)90}$

$6\overline{)57}$ $\qquad$ $8\overline{)44}$ $\qquad$ $5\overline{)58}$ $\qquad$ $6\overline{)21}$

Write the answers to these sums choosing decimal or fraction remainders.

$6\overline{)15}$ $\qquad$ $8\overline{)60}$ $\qquad$ $8\overline{)26}$ $\qquad$ $6\overline{)27}$

$6\overline{)33}$ $\qquad$ $8\overline{)36}$ $\qquad$ $5\overline{)92}$ $\qquad$ $5\overline{)59}$

Division of 3-digit decimal numbers

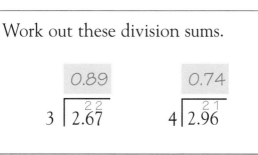

Work out these division sums.

$$0.89$$
$$3 \overline{)2.\overset{2\,2}{6}7}$$

$$0.74$$
$$4 \overline{)2.\overset{2\,1}{9}6}$$

Work out these division sums.

$$3 \overline{)2.22}$$ $$4 \overline{)7.32}$$ $$4 \overline{)6.12}$$ $$2 \overline{)3.24}$$

$$2 \overline{)9.98}$$ $$3 \overline{)9.72}$$ $$3 \overline{)2.61}$$ $$4 \overline{)7.48}$$

$$4 \overline{)2.24}$$ $$2 \overline{)2.94}$$ $$3 \overline{)2.25}$$ $$4 \overline{)6.24}$$

$$4 \overline{)5.56}$$ $$2 \overline{)8.66}$$ $$2 \overline{)7.88}$$ $$3 \overline{)7.32}$$

$$4 \overline{)8.64}$$ $$2 \overline{)8.96}$$ $$3 \overline{)8.55}$$ $$4 \overline{)9.84}$$

Write the answer in the box.

What is 8.56 divided by 4?

What is $\frac{1}{3}$ of 2.64?

What is 9.45 divided by 3?

What is $\frac{1}{4}$ of 2.72?

Share 7.92 equally among 4.

Halve 6.94.

Work out the answer to each sum.

£2.64 is shared equally among four people.
How much do they each get?

A piece of wood is 9.48 metres long and is cut
into three equal pieces. How long is each piece?

Division of 3-digit decimal numbers

Work out these division sums.

$$\begin{array}{r} 1.99 \\ \hline 5\,|\,9.95 \\ {\scriptstyle 44} \end{array}$$

$$\begin{array}{r} 1.61 \\ \hline 6\,|\,9.66 \\ {\scriptstyle 3} \end{array}$$

Work out these division sums.

5 | 8.15   5 | 9.25   5 | 6.35   6 | 6.36

6 | 2.16   7 | 8.82   7 | 4.83   8 | 5.92

8 | 8.72   9 | 8.19   9 | 5.67   6 | 9.12

6 | 5.94   8 | 8.48   7 | 2.66   7 | 9.45

9 | 7.56   8 | 9.44   7 | 4.27   7 | 9.17

Write the answer in the box.

What is 8.82 divided by 9?

Find $\frac{1}{8}$ of 9.28

What is 8.22 divided by 6?

Find $\frac{1}{9}$ of 5.85

Share 3.78 equally among 6

What is 3.12 divided by 8?

Work out the answer to each sum.

Sammy spends £2.85 a week on his bus fares to school. How much is his bus fare each day?

A fence is 9.48 metres long. If it is made up of 6 panels, how long is each panel?

Real-life problems

A family is driving 120 km to visit friends. If they have already driven 30% of the distance, how far have they travelled?

$$\frac{120 \times 30}{100} =$$ 36 km

Mr Chang gets a £500 bonus from his firm. He puts 40% in the bank and spends the rest. How much does he put in the bank?

How much does he spend?

A school has 300 children. 55% of them are girls. How many boys are there in the school?

In a spelling test of 80 words Sinead gets 75% right. How many does she get wrong?

A man wins £5,000 on the lottery. If he gives 25% to charity, how much does he keep for himself?

A man has to drive 240 km to get home from a business trip. If he has driven 35% of the journey, how much further does he have to go?

Cyril's house cost £96,000. James's house cost 10% less. How much did James's house cost?

Reading from scales

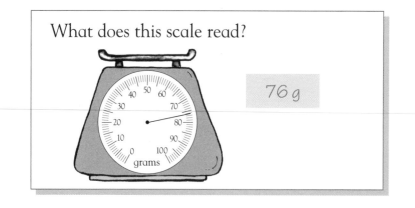

What does this scale read?

76 g

What do these scales read?

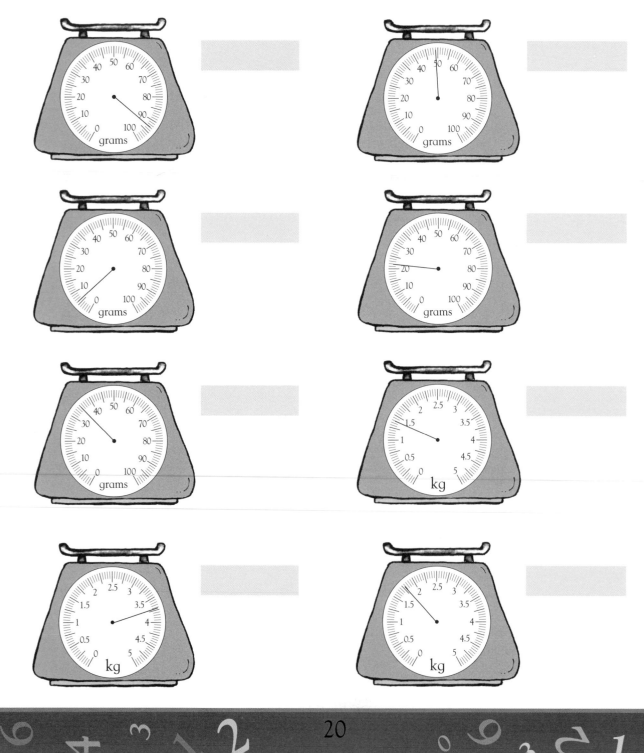

Mean, median, and mode

Sian throws a dice 7 times. Here are her results:

4, 2, 1, 2, 4, 2, 6

What is the mean? $(4 + 2 + 1 + 2 + 4 + 2 + 6) \div 7 = 3$

What is the median?   Put the numbers in order of size and find the middle number, e.g., 1, 2, 2, 2, 4, 4, 6.

The median is 2.

What is the mode?   The most common result, which is 2.

A school football team scores the following number of goals in their first 9 matches:
2, 2, 1, 3, 2, 1, 2, 4, 1

What is the mean score?

What is the median score?

Write down the mode for their results.

The ages of a local hockey team were:
17, 15, 16, 19, 17, 19, 22, 17, 18, 21, 17

What is the mean of their ages?

What is their median age?

Write down the mode for their ages.

The results of Susan's last 11 spelling tests were:
15, 12, 15, 17, 11, 16, 19, 11, 3, 11, 13

What is the mean of her scores?

What is her median score?

Write down the mode for her scores.

11
13
11   12
3

Area of compound shapes

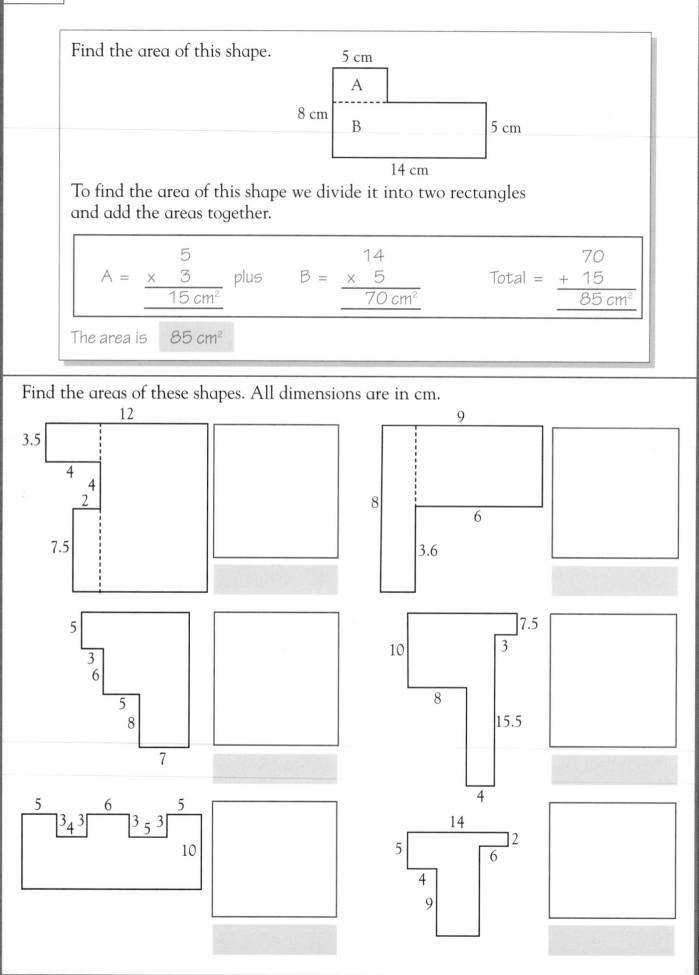

Find the area of this shape.

5 cm

A

8 cm

B

5 cm

14 cm

To find the area of this shape we divide it into two rectangles and add the areas together.

A = $\frac{5 \times 3}{15 \text{ cm}^2}$ plus   B = $\frac{14 \times 5}{70 \text{ cm}^2}$ Total = $\frac{70 + 15}{85 \text{ cm}^2}$

The area is   85 cm²

Find the areas of these shapes. All dimensions are in cm.

12
3.5
4
4
2
7.5

9
8
6
3.6

5
3
6
5
8
7

10
7.5
3
8
15.5
4

5   6   5
3 4 3   3 5 3
10

14
5   2
6
4
9

Area of compound shapes

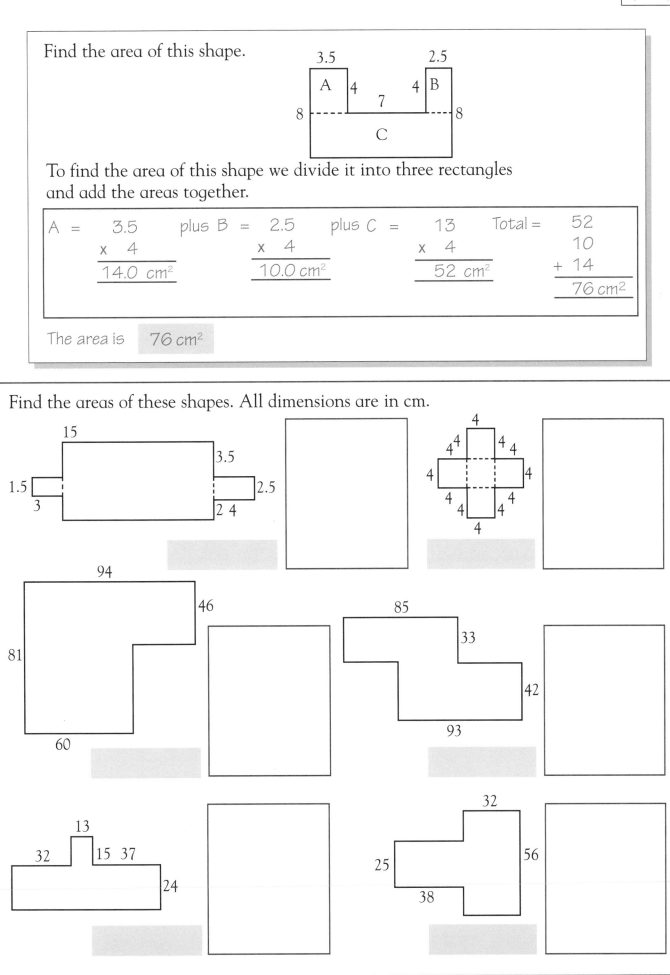

Find the area of this shape.

To find the area of this shape we divide it into three rectangles and add the areas together.

A =	3.5	plus B =	2.5	plus C =	13	Total =	52
	x 4		x 4		x 4		10
	14.0 cm²		10.0 cm²		52 cm²		+ 14
							76 cm²

The area is   76 cm²

Find the areas of these shapes. All dimensions are in cm.

Surface area of cuboids

Find the surface area of this cuboid.

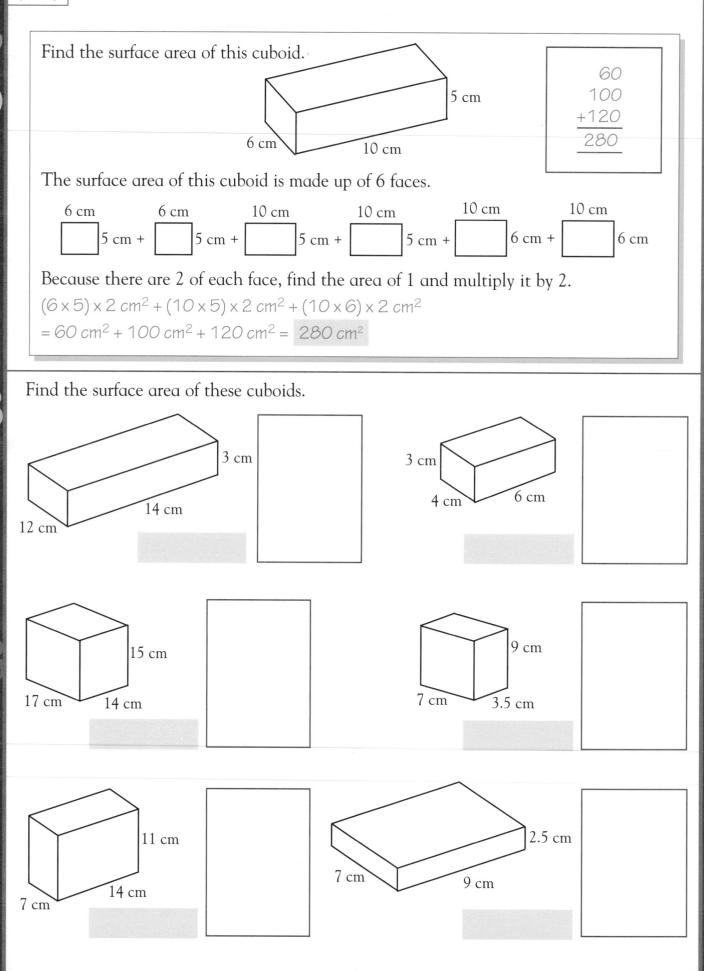

5 cm

6 cm   10 cm

$$\begin{array}{r} 60 \\ 100 \\ +120 \\ \hline 280 \end{array}$$

The surface area of this cuboid is made up of 6 faces.

6 cm   6 cm   10 cm   10 cm   10 cm   10 cm

☐ 5 cm +   ☐ 5 cm +   ☐ 5 cm +   ☐ 5 cm +   ☐ 6 cm +   ☐ 6 cm

Because there are 2 of each face, find the area of 1 and multiply it by 2.

$(6 \times 5) \times 2 \ cm^2 + (10 \times 5) \times 2 \ cm^2 + (10 \times 6) \times 2 \ cm^2$

$= 60 \ cm^2 + 100 \ cm^2 + 120 \ cm^2 = \boxed{280 \ cm^2}$

Find the surface area of these cuboids.

3 cm

14 cm

12 cm

3 cm   6 cm

4 cm

15 cm

17 cm   14 cm

9 cm

7 cm   3.5 cm

11 cm

14 cm

7 cm

2.5 cm

7 cm   9 cm

24

Surface area of cubes

Find the surface area of this cube.

6 cm

6 cm

6 cm

$(6 \times 6) \times 6$
$= 36 \times 6$

$\begin{array}{r} 36 \\ \times 6 \\ \hline 216 \end{array}$

Like the cuboid, the surface area of the cube is made up of 6 faces.

6 cm

6 cm +

6 cm

6 cm +

6 cm

6 cm +

6 cm

6 cm +

6 cm

6 cm +

6 cm

6 cm

Because the 6 faces are the same,
find the area of 1 and multiply it by 6.

216 cm²

Find the surface area of these cubes.

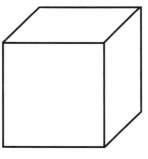

9 cm

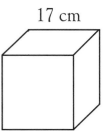

15 cm

24 cm

17 cm

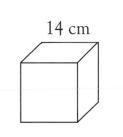

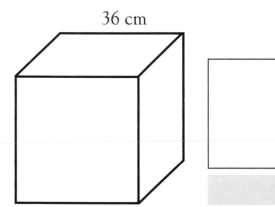

36 cm

14 cm

Nets of 3D shapes

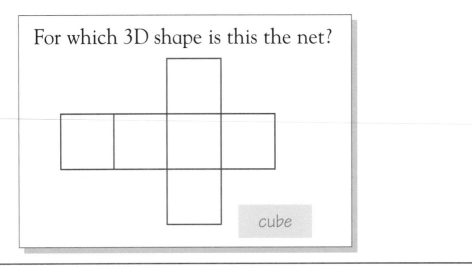

For which 3D shape is this the net?

cube

For which 3D shapes are these the nets?

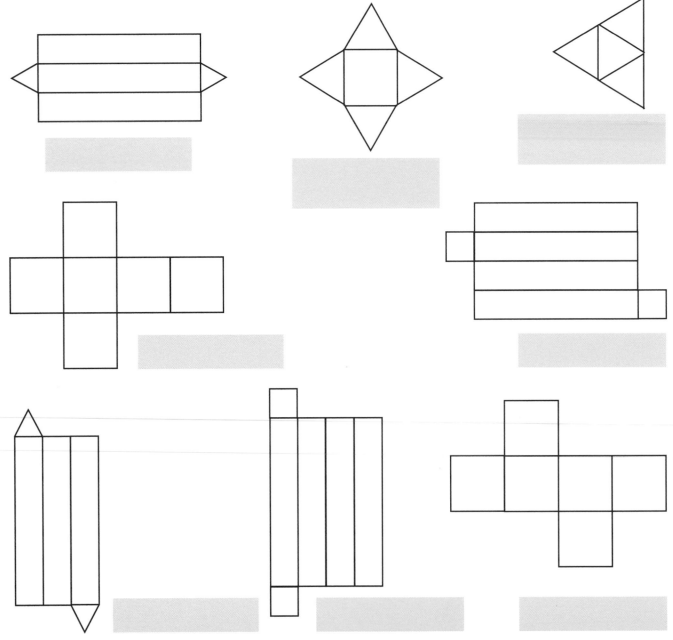

Nets of simple shapes

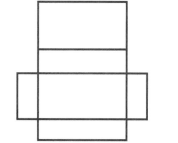

Sketch the net of this cuboid.

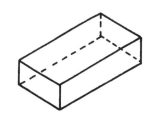

Sketch the nets of these shapes.

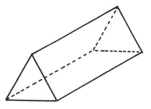

Triangular prism

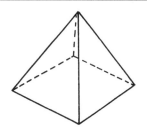

Square-based pyramid

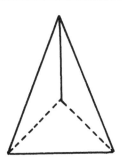

Triangular-based pyramid

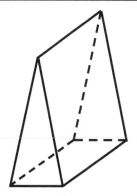

Triangular prism

More nets of simple shapes

★

Sketch the net of this rectangular pyramid.

Remember that sometimes a shape has more than 1 net.

Sketch the net of this cuboid.

Sketch the net of this cube.

Now sketch another two different nets of a cube.

Co-ordinates

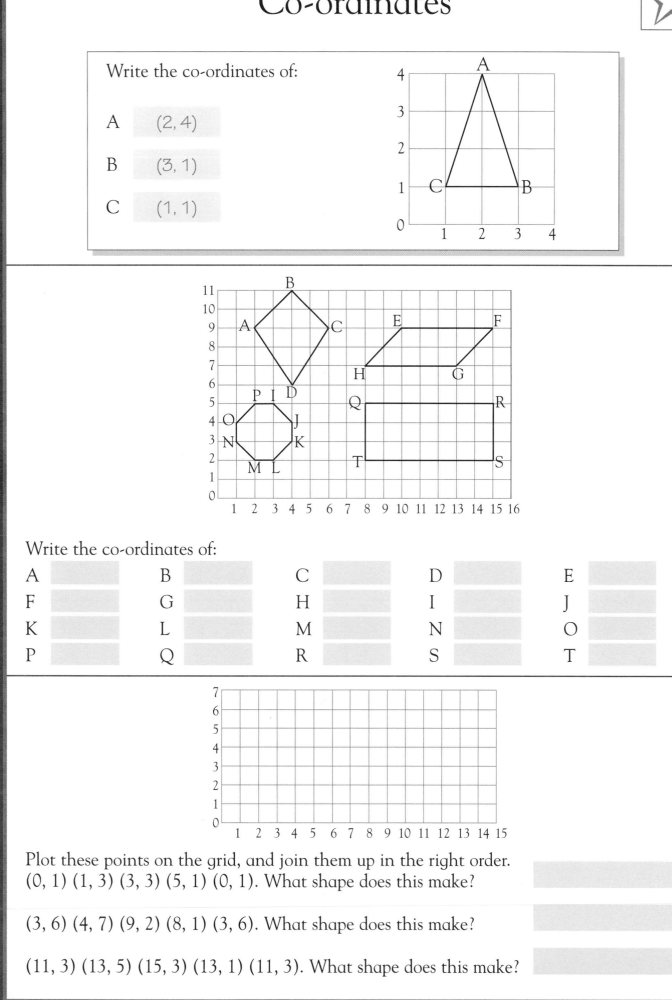

Write the co-ordinates of:

A   (2, 4)

B   (3, 1)

C   (1, 1)

Write the co-ordinates of:

A		B		C		D		E	
F		G		H		I		J	
K		L		M		N		O	
P		Q		R		S		T	

Plot these points on the grid, and join them up in the right order.
(0, 1) (1, 3) (3, 3) (5, 1) (0, 1). What shape does this make?

(3, 6) (4, 7) (9, 2) (8, 1) (3, 6). What shape does this make?

(11, 3) (13, 5) (15, 3) (13, 1) (11, 3). What shape does this make?

Drawing angles including reflex

Acute angles are between 0° and 90°.   Obtuse angles are between 90° and 180°.

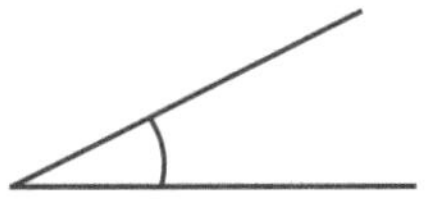

When you get to 180°
you have a straight line.

Reflex angles are bigger
than 180° and less than 360°.

Because reflex angles are bigger than 180°
you may find it easier to use a circular protractor in order to draw them.

Use a protractor to draw these angles. Remember to mark the angle you have drawn.

150°

135°

210°

350°

10°

20°

Drawing more angles including reflex

☆

Draw these angles. Remember to mark the angle you have drawn.

275°	65°
330°	35°
25°	345°
165°	5°

Find the angle

⭐

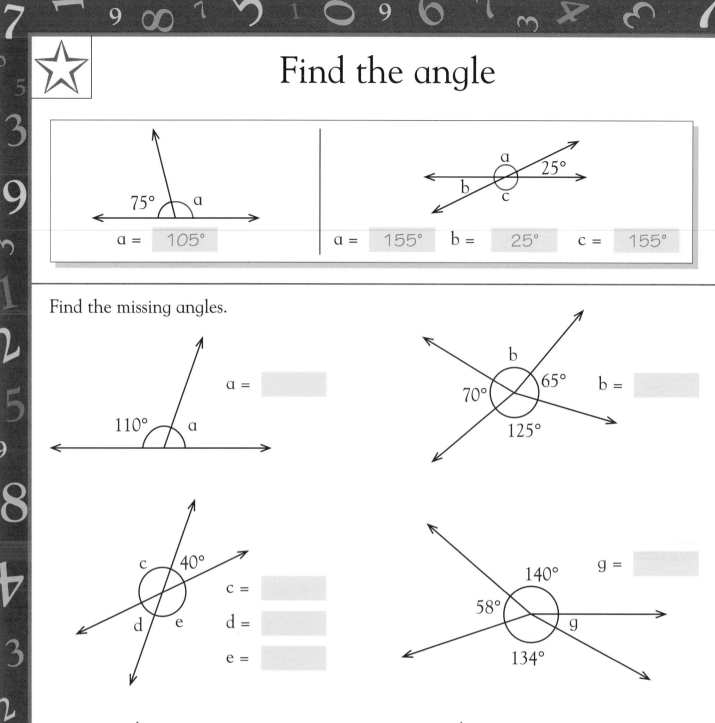

a = **105°**

a = **155°**   b = **25°**   c = **155°**

Find the missing angles.

a =

b =

c =

d =

e =

g =

a =

b =

a =

d =

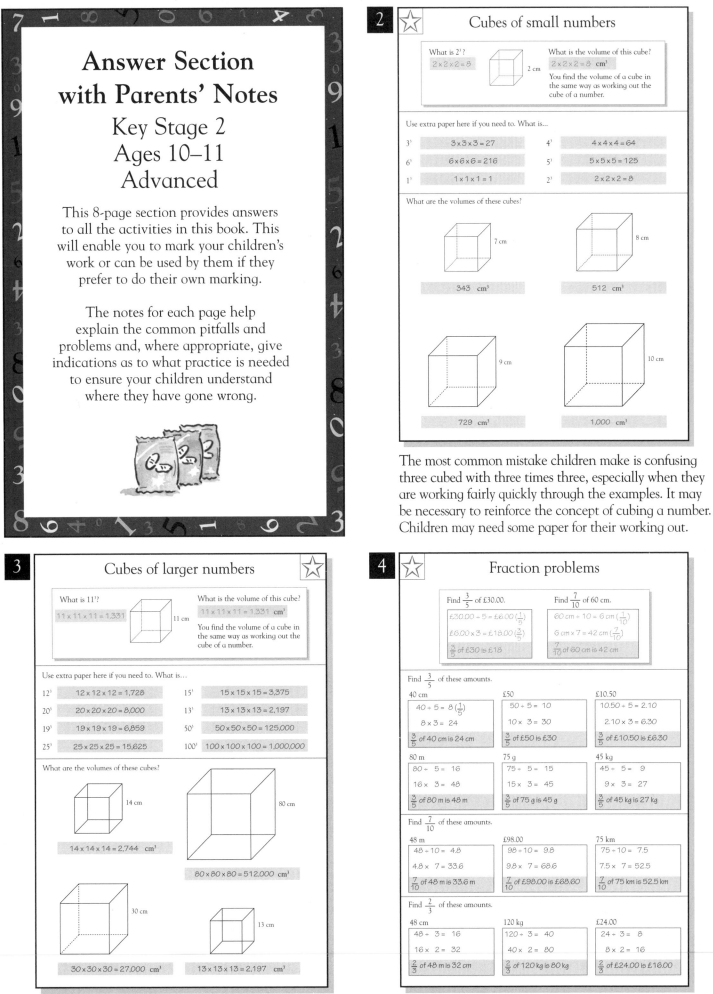

Answer Section with Parents' Notes
Key Stage 2
Ages 10–11
Advanced

This 8-page section provides answers to all the activities in this book. This will enable you to mark your children's work or can be used by them if they prefer to do their own marking.

The notes for each page help explain the common pitfalls and problems and, where appropriate, give indications as to what practice is needed to ensure your children understand where they have gone wrong.

2

Cubes of small numbers

What is 2^3?
$2 \times 2 \times 2 = 8$

What is the volume of this cube?
$2 \times 2 \times 2 = 8$ cm³

2 cm

You find the volume of a cube in the same way as working out the cube of a number.

Use extra paper here if you need to. What is...

3^3 $3 \times 3 \times 3 = 27$ 4^3 $4 \times 4 \times 4 = 64$

6^3 $6 \times 6 \times 6 = 216$ 5^3 $5 \times 5 \times 5 = 125$

1^3 $1 \times 1 \times 1 = 1$ 2^3 $2 \times 2 \times 2 = 8$

What are the volumes of these cubes?

7 cm → 343 cm³

8 cm → 512 cm³

9 cm → 729 cm³

10 cm → 1,000 cm³

The most common mistake children make is confusing three cubed with three times three, especially when they are working fairly quickly through the examples. It may be necessary to reinforce the concept of cubing a number. Children may need some paper for their working out.

3

Cubes of larger numbers

What is 11^3?
$11 \times 11 \times 11 = 1,331$

What is the volume of this cube?
$11 \times 11 \times 11 = 1,331$ cm³

11 cm

You find the volume of a cube in the same way as working out the cube of a number.

Use extra paper here if you need to. What is...

12^3 $12 \times 12 \times 12 = 1,728$ 15^3 $15 \times 15 \times 15 = 3,375$

20^3 $20 \times 20 \times 20 = 8,000$ 13^3 $13 \times 13 \times 13 = 2,197$

19^3 $19 \times 19 \times 19 = 6,859$ 50^3 $50 \times 50 \times 50 = 125,000$

25^3 $25 \times 25 \times 25 = 15,625$ 100^3 $100 \times 100 \times 100 = 1,000,000$

What are the volumes of these cubes?

14 cm → $14 \times 14 \times 14 = 2,744$ cm³

80 cm → $80 \times 80 \times 80 = 512,000$ cm³

30 cm → $30 \times 30 \times 30 = 27,000$ cm³

13 cm → $13 \times 13 \times 13 = 2,197$ cm³

This page extends the mathematical calculations to involve larger numbers, so long multiplication will be required. Children may need some paper for their working out. Some children may look at such numbers as 50^3, 30^3, and 80^3 and compare them to 5^3, 3^3, and 8^3.

4

Fraction problems

Find $\frac{3}{5}$ of £30.00.
$£30.00 \div 5 = £6.00 \left(\frac{1}{5}\right)$
$£6.00 \times 3 = £18.00 \left(\frac{3}{5}\right)$
$\frac{3}{5}$ of £30 is £18

Find $\frac{7}{10}$ of 60 cm.
$60 \text{ cm} \div 10 = 6 \text{ cm} \left(\frac{1}{10}\right)$
$6 \text{ cm} \times 7 = 42 \text{ cm} \left(\frac{7}{10}\right)$
$\frac{7}{10}$ of 60 cm is 42 cm

Find $\frac{3}{5}$ of these amounts.

40 cm
$40 \div 5 = 8 \left(\frac{1}{5}\right)$
$8 \times 3 = 24$
$\frac{3}{5}$ of 40 cm is 24 cm

£50
$50 \div 5 = 10$
$10 \times 3 = 30$
$\frac{3}{5}$ of £50 is £30

£10.50
$10.50 \div 5 = 2.10$
$2.10 \times 3 = 6.30$
$\frac{3}{5}$ of £10.50 is £6.30

80 m
$80 \div 5 = 16$
$16 \times 3 = 48$
$\frac{3}{5}$ of 80 m is 48 m

75 g
$75 \div 5 = 15$
$15 \times 3 = 45$
$\frac{3}{5}$ of 75 g is 45 g

45 kg
$45 \div 5 = 9$
$9 \times 3 = 27$
$\frac{3}{5}$ of 45 kg is 27 kg

Find $\frac{7}{10}$ of these amounts.

48 m
$48 \div 10 = 4.8$
$4.8 \times 7 = 33.6$
$\frac{7}{10}$ of 48 m is 33.6 m

£98.00
$98 \div 10 = 9.8$
$9.8 \times 7 = 68.6$
$\frac{7}{10}$ of £98.00 is £68.60

75 km
$75 \div 10 = 7.5$
$7.5 \times 7 = 52.5$
$\frac{7}{10}$ of 75 km is 52.5 km

Find $\frac{2}{3}$ of these amounts.

48 cm
$48 \div 3 = 16$
$16 \times 2 = 32$
$\frac{2}{3}$ of 48 m is 32 cm

120 kg
$120 \div 3 = 40$
$40 \times 2 = 80$
$\frac{2}{3}$ of 120 kg is 80 kg

£24.00
$24 \div 3 = 8$
$8 \times 2 = 16$
$\frac{2}{3}$ of £24.00 is £16.00

Ensure that children are dividing the amount by the denominator and multiplying the result by the numerator. You could explain that we divide by the bottom to find one part and multiply by the top to find the number of parts we want.

5 — Finding percentages

Find 30% of 140.

(Divide by 100 to find 1% and then multiply by 30 to find 30%.) $\frac{140}{100} \times 30 = 42$

Find 12% of 75. $\frac{75^3}{100} \times \frac{3}{12} = 9$

Find 30% of these numbers.

620   $\frac{620}{100} \times 30 = 186$ 240 $\frac{240}{100} \times 30 = 72$

80   $\frac{80}{100} \times 30 = 24$ 160 $\frac{160}{100} \times 30 = 48$

Find 60% of these numbers.

60   $\frac{60}{100} \times 60 = 36$ 100 $\frac{100}{100} \times 60 = 60$

160   $\frac{160}{100} \times 60 = 96$ 580 $\frac{580}{100} \times 60 = 348$

Find 45% of these amounts.

80 g $\frac{80^4}{100} \times 45 = 36\,g$ 40 cm $\frac{40^2}{100} \times 45 = 18\,cm$

240 ml $\frac{240^{12}}{100} \times 45 = 108\,ml$ 600 km $\frac{600^{30}}{100} \times 45 = 270\,km$

Find 12% of these amounts.

£150 $\frac{150}{100} \times 12 = £18$ £600 $\frac{600}{100} \times 12 = £72$

125 m $\frac{125}{100} \times 12 = 15\,m$ 775 m $\frac{775}{100} \times 12 = 93\,m$

The most common error when finding percentages is to reverse the operation, i.e., to divide by the percentage required and multiply by 100. Explain again that if the whole is 100% we divide the number by 100 to find 1% and then multiply by the percentage we want.

6 — Factors, multiples, and prime numbers

Write all the factors of these numbers.

12   1, 2, 3, 4, 6, 12   18   1, 2, 3, 6, 9, 18

25   1, 5, 25   64   1, 2, 4, 8, 16, 32, 64

72   1, 2, 3, 4, 6, 8, 9, 12, 18, 24, 36, 72   96   1, 2, 3, 4, 6, 8, 12, 16, 24, 32, 48, 96

What are the common factors of these numbers?

15 and 25   1, 5

72 and 108   1, 2, 3, 4, 6, 9, 12, 18, 36

48 and 64   1, 2, 4, 8, 16

150 and 125   1, 5, 25

Circle the multiples of these numbers.

Multiples of 3   ⑨   ⑮   26   ㉝   62

Multiples of 5   17   ㉕   43   ⑦⓪   ⑨⑤

Multiples of 8   26   ㉜   ㊗   62   ⑨⑥

Write the first three common multiples of these numbers.

3 and 5   15, 30, 45

4 and 7   28, 56, 84

Write the prime numbers between these numbers.

1 and 20   2, 3, 5, 7, 11, 13, 17, 19

20 and 50   23, 29, 31, 37, 41, 43, 47

Knowing common factors and multiples helps in finding equivalent fractions. The activities reinforce familiarity with times tables, division, and multiplication. Check that your child understands that a prime number is always greater than 1 and has no other factors except 1 and itself.

7 — Add and subtract fractions

Work out these sums.

$\frac{1}{4} + \frac{5}{6} = \frac{3}{12} + \frac{10}{12} = \frac{13}{12} = 1\frac{1}{12}$

$\frac{7}{9} - \frac{2}{3} = \frac{7}{9} - \frac{6}{9} = \frac{1}{9}$

Remember: Use equivalent fractions to make the denominators the same.

Add these fractions. Give answers as improper fractions if necessary.

$\frac{1}{3} + \frac{1}{3} = \frac{2}{3}$ $\frac{4}{11} + \frac{3}{4} = \frac{49}{44}$ $\frac{6}{9} + \frac{12}{18} = \frac{24}{18}$ $\frac{3}{5} + \frac{4}{10} = \frac{10}{10}$

$\frac{3}{8} + \frac{2}{8} = \frac{5}{8}$ $\frac{1}{5} + \frac{3}{5} = \frac{4}{5}$ $\frac{2}{5} + \frac{6}{15} = \frac{12}{15}$ $\frac{4}{7} + \frac{2}{5} = \frac{34}{35}$

$\frac{2}{6} + \frac{3}{12} = \frac{7}{12}$ $\frac{5}{9} + \frac{3}{9} = \frac{8}{9}$ $\frac{2}{7} + \frac{4}{7} = \frac{6}{7}$ $\frac{2}{5} + \frac{3}{9} = \frac{33}{45}$

$\frac{5}{12} + \frac{4}{12} = \frac{23}{24}$ $\frac{1}{4} + \frac{3}{8} = \frac{5}{8}$ $\frac{4}{10} + \frac{3}{10} = \frac{7}{10}$

Add these mixed fractions. Give answers as mixed fractions.
Remember: First change them to improper fractions.

$1\frac{1}{4} + 3\frac{1}{4} = 4\frac{1}{2}$ $3\frac{1}{3} + 4\frac{1}{2} = 7\frac{5}{6}$ $2\frac{2}{5} + 2\frac{3}{5} = 5$

$2\frac{3}{4} + 1\frac{2}{3} = 4\frac{5}{12}$ $1\frac{4}{5} + 3\frac{3}{10} = 5\frac{1}{10}$ $4\frac{5}{8} + 2\frac{3}{4} = 7\frac{3}{8}$

Subtract these fractions. Write answers in simplest form.

$\frac{3}{5} - \frac{2}{5} = \frac{1}{5}$ $\frac{3}{4} - \frac{7}{12} = \frac{1}{6}$ $\frac{3}{5} - \frac{1}{3} = \frac{4}{15}$ $\frac{1}{3} - \frac{1}{4} = \frac{1}{12}$

$\frac{4}{5} - \frac{7}{10} = \frac{1}{10}$ $\frac{5}{8} - \frac{3}{8} = \frac{1}{4}$ $\frac{11}{15} - \frac{2}{5} = \frac{1}{3}$ $\frac{1}{2} - \frac{2}{7} = \frac{3}{14}$

$\frac{2}{3} - \frac{4}{9} = \frac{2}{9}$ $\frac{5}{6} - \frac{2}{3} = \frac{1}{6}$ $\frac{7}{9} - \frac{2}{9} = \frac{5}{9}$ $\frac{1}{2} - \frac{5}{12} = \frac{1}{12}$

Subtract these mixed fractions. Give answers in simplest form.
Remember: First change them to improper fractions.

$4\frac{2}{5} - 3\frac{4}{5} = \frac{3}{5}$ $2\frac{5}{8} - 1\frac{7}{8} = \frac{3}{4}$ $5\frac{4}{9} - 4\frac{2}{9} = 1\frac{2}{9}$

$2\frac{2}{3} - 1\frac{3}{4} = \frac{11}{12}$ $2\frac{1}{2} - 2\frac{3}{8} = \frac{1}{8}$ $4\frac{5}{6} - 3\frac{2}{3} = 1\frac{1}{6}$

Knowledge of equivalent fractions is needed to make the denominators the same while adding and subtracting fractions. Your child should use common multiples to make fractions with the same denominators and also be confident in writing simple, improper, and mixed fractions.

8 — Multiply fractions

Work out these sums.

$\frac{2}{3} \times \frac{1}{2} = \frac{2 \times 1}{3 \times 2} = \frac{2}{6} = \frac{1}{3}$

$\frac{2}{5} \times 2 = \frac{2}{5} \times \frac{2}{1} = \frac{2 \times 2}{5 \times 1} = \frac{4}{5}$

Multiply these fractions. Give answers in their simplest form.

$\frac{3}{4} \times \frac{1}{2} = \frac{3}{8}$ $\frac{3}{5} \times \frac{2}{3} = \frac{2}{5}$

$\frac{3}{10} \times \frac{2}{5} = \frac{3}{25}$ $\frac{1}{2} \times \frac{3}{7} = \frac{3}{14}$

$\frac{2}{3} \times \frac{1}{4} = \frac{1}{6}$ $\frac{5}{8} \times \frac{2}{4} = \frac{5}{16}$

$\frac{7}{10} \times \frac{3}{4} = \frac{21}{40}$ $\frac{1}{2} \times \frac{5}{8} = \frac{5}{16}$

$\frac{2}{3} \times \frac{4}{10} = \frac{4}{15}$ $\frac{3}{5} \times \frac{2}{6} = \frac{1}{5}$

$\frac{4}{9} \times \frac{1}{3} = \frac{4}{27}$ $\frac{2}{3} \times \frac{5}{6} = \frac{5}{9}$

Multiply these fractions by whole numbers. Give answers as mixed fractions.

$\frac{2}{3} \times 4 = 2\frac{2}{3}$ $\frac{3}{5} \times 2 = 1\frac{1}{5}$

$\frac{3}{4} \times 6 = 4\frac{1}{2}$ $\frac{3}{10} \times 5 = 1\frac{1}{2}$

$\frac{5}{8} \times 3 = 1\frac{7}{8}$ $\frac{4}{7} \times 8 = 4\frac{4}{7}$

$\frac{1}{5} \times 9 = 1\frac{4}{5}$ $\frac{1}{4} \times 4 = 1$

$\frac{5}{12} \times 3 = 1\frac{1}{4}$ $\frac{6}{11} \times 2 = 1\frac{1}{11}$

$\frac{5}{9} \times 3 = 1\frac{2}{3}$ $\frac{10}{100} \times 4 = \frac{2}{5}$

Children may be taught using a variety of images such as pizzas. For example, $\frac{2}{3}$ of a pizza when each third is halved becomes $\frac{1}{3}$. The answers are given in their simplest forms to encourage your child to check that the fractions cannot be reduced further.

Divide fractions ⭐

Work out these sums.

$$\frac{1}{3} \div 2 = \frac{1}{3} \div \frac{2}{1} = \frac{1}{3} \times \frac{1}{2} = \frac{1}{6}$$

$$\frac{4}{7} \div \frac{3}{5} = \frac{4}{7} \times \frac{5}{3} = \frac{4 \times 5}{7 \times 3} = \frac{20}{21}$$

Divide these fractions by whole numbers. Give answers in their simplest form.

$\frac{1}{3} \div 3 = \boxed{\frac{1}{9}}$ $\qquad$ $\frac{4}{5} \div 2 = \boxed{\frac{2}{5}}$

$\frac{3}{8} \div 2 = \boxed{\frac{3}{16}}$ $\qquad$ $\frac{1}{4} \div 6 = \boxed{\frac{1}{24}}$

$\frac{1}{2} \div 5 = \boxed{\frac{1}{10}}$ $\qquad$ $\frac{3}{4} \div 7 = \boxed{\frac{3}{28}}$

$\frac{7}{10} \div 3 = \boxed{\frac{7}{30}}$ $\qquad$ $\frac{2}{9} \div 5 = \boxed{\frac{2}{45}}$

$\frac{3}{7} \div 3 = \boxed{\frac{1}{7}}$ $\qquad$ $\frac{2}{5} \div 4 = \boxed{\frac{1}{10}}$

$\frac{2}{3} \div 6 = \boxed{\frac{1}{9}}$ $\qquad$ $\frac{5}{6} \div 3 = \boxed{\frac{5}{18}}$

Divide these fractions. Give answers as a mixed number if needed.

$\frac{1}{2} \div \frac{1}{3} = \boxed{1\frac{1}{2}}$ $\qquad$ $\frac{3}{4} \div \frac{2}{3} = \boxed{1\frac{1}{8}}$

$\frac{3}{5} \div \frac{1}{6} = \boxed{3\frac{3}{5}}$ $\qquad$ $\frac{5}{7} \div \frac{2}{5} = \boxed{1\frac{11}{14}}$

$\frac{2}{9} \div \frac{3}{5} = \boxed{\frac{10}{27}}$ $\qquad$ $\frac{5}{8} \div \frac{1}{2} = \boxed{1\frac{1}{4}}$

$\frac{7}{10} \div \frac{1}{4} = \boxed{2\frac{4}{5}}$ $\qquad$ $\frac{3}{7} \div \frac{4}{9} = \boxed{\frac{27}{28}}$

$\frac{4}{5} \div \frac{5}{6} = \boxed{\frac{24}{25}}$ $\qquad$ $\frac{1}{4} \div \frac{3}{10} = \boxed{\frac{5}{6}}$

$\frac{2}{5} \div \frac{1}{3} = \boxed{1\frac{1}{5}}$ $\qquad$ $\frac{1}{8} \div \frac{9}{10} = \boxed{\frac{5}{36}}$

When dividing fractions, children need to get used to swapping around the numerator and denominator of the second fraction given to create a multiplication sum. Whole numbers are always made into improper fractions when calculating with fractions.

⭐ Ratio and proportion

A rat has 7 babies every 4 months.
How many babies does the rat have in one year? — 21

In a class, there are 2 girls for every 3 boys.
There are 10 girls. How many boys are there? — 15 boys

In a week, a dog eats 4 cans of dog food with 7 biscuits.
How many biscuits are needed for 24 cans? — 42 biscuits

A cook uses 6 apples with 300 g flour to make an apple crumble. How many apples are needed with 1.5 kg of flour? — 30 apples

In a bathroom, a black tile is used for every 5 white tiles.
How many black tiles are needed for 60 white tiles? — 12 black tiles

An account earns £2.50 interest for every £10,000 saved.
How much interest is earned on £150,000? — £37.50

A rectangle is drawn with length 5 cm x width 8 cm.
If it is drawn 4 times larger with length 20 cm, what is the width? — 32 cm

A model of a building uses the scale 10 cm = 200 ft.
The model of the building is 75 cm high. What is the actual height going to be? — 1,500 ft

A good understanding of ratio and proportions helps when comparing sizes and scales, and working out quantities in the same ratio, such as for recipes and shapes. Practical real-life problems encourage children to see how this understanding can be applied.

Algebra ⭐

Work out this equation.

$a + 5 = 7$
$a + 5\,(-5) = 7\,(-5)$
$a = 2$

$10 - b = 4$
$10 - b\,(+b) = 4\,(+b)$
$10\,(-4) = 4 + b\,(-4)$
$b = 6$

$a + 4 = 14 - 6$
$a + 4 = 8$
$a + 4\,(-4) = 8\,(-4)$
$a = 4$

Find value of each letter.

$a + 6 = 24$ $\boxed{a = 18}$ $\qquad$ $b - 5 = 14$ $\boxed{b = 19}$

$a + 28 = 42$ $\boxed{a = 14}$ $\qquad$ $b - 17 = 17$ $\boxed{b = 34}$

$a + 17 = 25$ $\boxed{a = 8}$ $\qquad$ $b - 27 = 23$ $\boxed{b = 50}$

$10 + y = 12$ $\boxed{y = 2}$ $\qquad$ $16 - x = 4$ $\boxed{x = 12}$

$38 + y = 50$ $\boxed{y = 12}$ $\qquad$ $26 - x = 9$ $\boxed{x = 17}$

$42 + y = 64$ $\boxed{y = 22}$ $\qquad$ $42 - x = 20$ $\boxed{x = 22}$

Solve these equations.

$15 + a = 42 - 17$ $\boxed{a = 10}$ $\qquad$ $y + 13 = 7 \times 5$ $\boxed{y = 22}$

$100 - b = 72 + 14$ $\boxed{b = 14}$ $\qquad$ $x - 42 = 96 \div 8$ $\boxed{x = 54}$

$63 + a = 9 \times 9$ $\boxed{a = 18}$ $\qquad$ $21 - y = 40 - 25$ $\boxed{y = 6}$

Write equations for these problems and then solve them.

Laura had a bookcase overloaded with books. She gave 24 to a school fair. She had 36 left. How many books did she have to begin with? — $b - 24 = 36$ so $b = 60$

Dan collected comics. He was given a set of 12 for his birthday. He now had 64 in his collection. How many comics did he have before his birthday? — $c + 12 = 64$ so $c = 52$

At this stage, children will be encouraged to start using letters and symbols in place of missing numbers in number problems. This letter or symbol is called the variable. When solving equations, your child needs to remember to perform the same operation to both sides to get the variable alone.

⭐ More algebra

Work out this equation.

$10 - a = a$
$10 - a\,(+a) = a\,(+a)$
$10 = 2a$
$10\,(\div 2) = 2a\,(\div 2)$
$a = 5$

$3b + 15 = 12 \times 6$
$3b + 15\,(-15) = 72\,(-15)$
$3b = 57$
$3b\,(\div 3) = 57\,(\div 3)$
$b = 19$

$27 \div c = 9$
$27 - c\,(\times c) = 9\,(\times c)$
$27 = 9c$
$27\,(\div 9) = 9c\,(\div 9)$
$c = 3$

Find value of each letter.

$5a = 25$ $\boxed{a = 5}$ $\qquad$ $15 \div c = 5$ $\boxed{c = 3}$

$a = 36 - a$ $\boxed{a = 18}$ $\qquad$ $32 \div c = 8$ $\boxed{c = 4}$

$6a = 42$ $\boxed{a = 7}$ $\qquad$ $56 \div c = 7$ $\boxed{c = 8}$

$3y + 8 = 20$ $\boxed{y = 4}$ $\qquad$ $d \div 4 = 7$ $\boxed{d = 28}$

$6y - 16 = 38$ $\boxed{y = 9}$ $\qquad$ $d \div 9 = 5$ $\boxed{d = 45}$

$42 - 5y = 22$ $\boxed{y = 4}$ $\qquad$ $d \div 11 = 10$ $\boxed{d = 110}$

Solve these equations.

$56 - a = 26 + 2a$ $\boxed{a = 10}$ $\qquad$ $48 \div d = 7 + 5$ $\boxed{d = 4}$

$2b + 16 = (12 \times 3) - 2$ $\boxed{b = 9}$ $\qquad$ $17 + c = 26 - 2c$ $\boxed{c = 3}$

$4y - 27 = 72 \div 8$ $\boxed{y = 9}$ $\qquad$ $4e + 45 = 35 + 6e$ $\boxed{e = 5}$

Write equations for these problems and then solve them.

Isla bought two packets of biscuits and a 20 pence bunch of bananas. The total cost was 80 pence. How much is one pack of biscuits? — $2b + 20 = 80$ so $b = 30$

Jodie invited 48 guests to her New Year party. 10 people couldn't make it and half of the rest were going to arrive late. How many were going to be on time? — $48 = 10 + 2g$ so $g = 19$

Children should know that $a + a + a = 3a$ or $3 \times a$. Encourage children to check that their answers are correct by inserting the number in place of the letter and then calculate each side of the equation to make sure the answer is the same.

13 — Multiplication by tens and units ☆

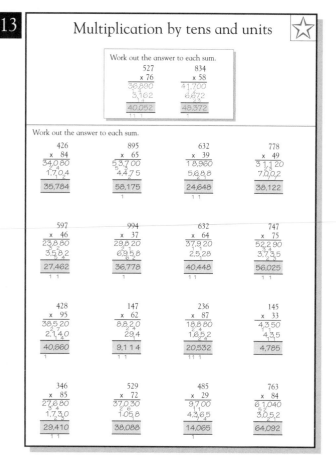

Work out the answer to each sum.

```
  527        834
x  76      x  58
36,890     41,700
 5,162      6,672
40,052     48,372
```

Work out the answer to each sum.

```
  426        895        632        778
x  84      x  65      x  39      x  49
34,080     53,700     18,960     31,120
 1,704      4,475      5,688      7,002
35,784     58,175     24,648     38,122
```

```
  597        994        632        747
x  46      x  37      x  64      x  75
23,880     29,820     37,920     52,290
 3,582      6,958      2,528      3,735
27,462     36,778     40,448     56,025
```

```
  428        147        236        145
x  95      x  62      x  87      x  33
38,520      8,820     18,880      4,350
 2,140        294      1,652        435
40,660      9,114     20,532      4,785
```

```
  346        529        485        763
x  85      x  72      x  29      x  84
27,680     37,030      9,700     61,040
 1,730      1,058      4,365      3,052
29,410     38,088     14,065     64,092
```

Explain that multiplying by 84 means multiplying by 80, then by 4, and then adding the answers together. Multiplying by 10 (or 80) means adding a nought and multiplying by 1 (8). Multiplying by the tens digit first saves having to remember to put the nought later.

14 — ☆ Multiplying decimals

Work out these sums.

```
 1.456     1.456     1.456     1.456
x   10    x   20    x    3    x   23
14.56     29.12     4.368     29.120
                             +4.368
                             33.488
```

Multiply these numbers.

```
 2.567     4.687      8.924     3.963
x   10    x   10     x  100    x  100
25.67     46.87      892.4     396.3
```

```
12.892     7.689      9.578    15.432
x  100    x 1,000    x 1,000   x 1,000
1,289.2    7,689      9,578    15,432
```

Multiply these numbers.

```
0.456     0.351      1.764     14.23
x   2     x   4      x   8     x   3
0.912     1.404     14.112     42.69
```

```
0.859     1.034      8.049     69.23
x   7     x   6      x   5     x   3
6.013     6.204     40.245    207.69
```

```
 2.836     0.765      5.218     62.73
x   12    x   18     x   30    x   45
28.360     7.650     156.54   2,509.20
+5.672    +6.120             +313.65
34.032    13.77              2,822.85
```

```
 1.873    20.72      708.7      8.302
x   60    x   21     x   15    x   40
112.38    415.40    7,087.0    332.08
          +20.72    +3,543.5
          435.12   10,630.5
```

When multiplying decimals, it is important to note where the decimal point goes. When multiplying by 10, 100, or 1,000, the decimal point moves as each number's value increases. When multiplying by whole numbers, encourage children to keep decimal points underneath each other.

15 — Division by units ☆

47÷2 can be written in two ways:

$$23\frac{1}{2} \quad \text{or} \quad 23.5$$
$$2\overline{)47} \qquad 2\overline{)47.0}$$

Write the answers to these sums with fraction remainders.

| $8\frac{1}{2}$ | $4\frac{3}{4}$ | $5\frac{1}{3}$ | $9\frac{1}{4}$ |
| $2\overline{)17}$ | $4\overline{)19}$ | $3\overline{)16}$ | $4\overline{)37}$ |

| $9\frac{2}{3}$ | $22\frac{1}{2}$ | $17\frac{2}{5}$ | $9\frac{4}{5}$ |
| $3\overline{)29}$ | $2\overline{)45}$ | $5\overline{)87}$ | $5\overline{)49}$ |

| $18\frac{1}{4}$ | $11\frac{2}{3}$ | $23\frac{1}{4}$ | $13\frac{4}{5}$ |
| $4\overline{)73}$ | $3\overline{)35}$ | $4\overline{)93}$ | $5\overline{)69}$ |

Write the answers to these sums with decimal remainders.

| 36.5 | 42.5 | 19.5 | 14.75 |
| $2\overline{)73}$ | $2\overline{)85}$ | $2\overline{)39}$ | $4\overline{)59}$ |

| 17.75 | 20.75 | 5.8 | 9.4 |
| $4\overline{)71}$ | $4\overline{)83}$ | $5\overline{)29}$ | $5\overline{)47}$ |

| 4.8 | 38.5 | 9.5 | 18.6 |
| $5\overline{)24}$ | $2\overline{)77}$ | $4\overline{)38}$ | $5\overline{)93}$ |

Write the answers to these sums choosing decimal or fraction remainders.

| 18.5 or $18\frac{1}{2}$ | 29.5 or $29\frac{1}{2}$ | 23.25 or $23\frac{1}{4}$ | 12.75 or $12\frac{3}{4}$ |
| $2\overline{)37}$ | $2\overline{)59}$ | $4\overline{)93}$ | $4\overline{)51}$ |

| 4.2 or $4\frac{1}{5}$ | 41.5 or $41\frac{1}{2}$ | 7.75 or $7\frac{3}{4}$ | 12.6 or $12\frac{3}{5}$ |
| $5\overline{)21}$ | $2\overline{)83}$ | $4\overline{)31}$ | $5\overline{)63}$ |

By now children will be comfortable with remainders. In the second section, they have to place a decimal point after the number being divided and add one or two noughts. Encourage them to use the last section as practice for the operation they found most difficult.

16 — ☆ More division by units

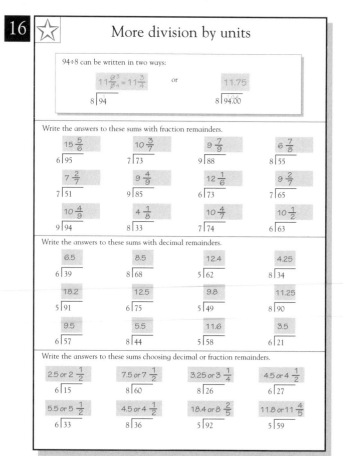

94÷8 can be written in two ways:

$$11\frac{6}{8} = 11\frac{3}{4} \quad \text{or} \quad 11.75$$
$$8\overline{)94} \qquad 8\overline{)94.00}$$

Write the answers to these sums with fraction remainders.

| $15\frac{5}{6}$ | $10\frac{3}{7}$ | $9\frac{7}{9}$ | $6\frac{7}{8}$ |
| $6\overline{)95}$ | $7\overline{)73}$ | $9\overline{)88}$ | $8\overline{)55}$ |

| $7\frac{2}{7}$ | $9\frac{4}{9}$ | $12\frac{1}{6}$ | $9\frac{2}{7}$ |
| $7\overline{)51}$ | $9\overline{)85}$ | $6\overline{)73}$ | $7\overline{)65}$ |

| $10\frac{4}{9}$ | $4\frac{1}{8}$ | $10\frac{4}{7}$ | $10\frac{1}{2}$ |
| $9\overline{)94}$ | $8\overline{)33}$ | $7\overline{)74}$ | $6\overline{)63}$ |

Write the answers to these sums with decimal remainders.

| 6.5 | 8.5 | 12.4 | 4.25 |
| $6\overline{)39}$ | $8\overline{)68}$ | $5\overline{)62}$ | $8\overline{)34}$ |

| 18.2 | 12.5 | 9.8 | 11.25 |
| $5\overline{)91}$ | $6\overline{)75}$ | $5\overline{)49}$ | $8\overline{)90}$ |

| 9.5 | 5.5 | 11.6 | 3.5 |
| $6\overline{)57}$ | $8\overline{)44}$ | $5\overline{)58}$ | $6\overline{)21}$ |

Write the answers to these sums choosing decimal or fraction remainders.

| 2.5 or $2\frac{1}{2}$ | 7.5 or $7\frac{1}{2}$ | 3.25 or $3\frac{1}{4}$ | 4.5 or $4\frac{1}{2}$ |
| $6\overline{)15}$ | $8\overline{)60}$ | $8\overline{)26}$ | $6\overline{)27}$ |

| 5.5 or $5\frac{1}{2}$ | 4.5 or $4\frac{1}{2}$ | 18.4 or $8\frac{2}{5}$ | 11.8 or $11\frac{4}{5}$ |
| $6\overline{)33}$ | $8\overline{)36}$ | $5\overline{)92}$ | $5\overline{)59}$ |

The comments on the previous page also apply to this one, but as the dividing numbers are larger any weaknesses in multiplication for the 6, 7, 8, and 9 times tables will show up. Simplifying some of the fraction answers is also required.

Division of 3-digit decimal numbers ☆

Work out these division sums.

$$3 \overline{)2.67} = 0.89 \qquad 4 \overline{)2.96} = 0.74$$

Work out these division sums.

$3\overline{)2.22} = 0.74$	$4\overline{)7.32} = 1.83$	$4\overline{)6.12} = 1.53$	$2\overline{)3.24} = 1.62$
$2\overline{)9.98} = 4.99$	$3\overline{)9.72} = 3.24$	$3\overline{)2.61} = 0.87$	$4\overline{)7.48} = 1.87$
$4\overline{)2.24} = 0.56$	$2\overline{)2.94} = 1.47$	$3\overline{)2.25} = 0.75$	$4\overline{)6.24} = 1.56$
$4\overline{)5.56} = 1.39$	$2\overline{)8.66} = 4.33$	$2\overline{)7.88} = 3.94$	$3\overline{)7.32} = 2.44$
$4\overline{)8.64} = 2.16$	$2\overline{)8.96} = 4.48$	$3\overline{)8.55} = 2.85$	$4\overline{)9.84} = 2.46$

Write the answer in the box.

What is 8.56 divided by 4? **2.14**   What is $\frac{1}{3}$ of 2.64? **0.88**

What is 9.45 divided by 3? **3.15**   What is $\frac{1}{4}$ of 2.72? **0.68**

Share 7.92 equally among 4. **1.98**   Halve 6.94. **3.47**

Work out the answer to each sum.

£2.64 is shared equally among four people. How much do they each get? **66 p**

A piece of wood is 9.48 metres long and is cut into three equal pieces. How long is each piece? **3.16 m**

On this page the decimal point has been incorporated into the middle of the number being divided. After the previous two pages, carrying across the decimal point should be familiar to children. No additional noughts need to be added on in this section.

Division of 3-digit decimal numbers

Work out these division sums.

$$5 \overline{)9.95} = 1.99 \qquad 6 \overline{)9.66} = 1.61$$

Work out these division sums.

$5\overline{)8.15} = 1.63$	$5\overline{)9.25} = 1.85$	$5\overline{)6.35} = 1.27$	$6\overline{)6.36} = 1.06$
$6\overline{)2.16} = 0.36$	$7\overline{)8.82} = 1.26$	$7\overline{)4.83} = 0.69$	$8\overline{)5.92} = 0.74$
$8\overline{)8.72} = 1.09$	$9\overline{)8.19} = 0.91$	$9\overline{)5.67} = 0.63$	$6\overline{)9.12} = 1.52$
$6\overline{)5.94} = 0.99$	$8\overline{)8.48} = 1.06$	$7\overline{)2.66} = 0.38$	$7\overline{)9.45} = 1.35$
$9\overline{)7.56} = 0.84$	$8\overline{)9.44} = 1.18$	$7\overline{)4.27} = 0.61$	$7\overline{)9.17} = 1.31$

Write the answer in the box.

What is 8.82 divided by 9? **0.98**   Find $\frac{1}{8}$ of 9.28 **1.16**

What is 8.22 divided by 6? **1.37**   Find $\frac{1}{9}$ of 5.85 **0.65**

Share 3.78 equally among 6 **0.63**   What is 3.12 divided by 8? **0.39**

Work out the answer to each sum.

Sammy spends £2.85 a week on his bus fares to school. How much is his bus fare each day? **57 p**

A fence is 9.48 metres long. If it is made up of 6 panels, how long is each panel? **1.58 m**

The comments on the previous page also apply to this one, but as the dividing numbers are larger any weaknesses in multiplication facts for 6, 7, 8, and 9 times tables will show up.

Real-life problems ☆

A family is driving 120 km to visit friends. If they have already driven 30% of the distance, how far have they travelled?

$$\frac{120 \times 30}{100} = \qquad \boxed{36 \text{ km}}$$

Mr Chang gets a £500 bonus from his firm. He puts 40% in the bank and spends the rest. How much does he put in the bank? **£200**

How much does he spend? **£300**

$$\frac{500 \times 40}{100} = 200$$
$$500 - 200 = 300$$

A school has 300 children. 55% of them are girls. How many boys are there in the school? **135 boys**

$$\frac{300 \times 45}{100} = 135$$

In a spelling test of 80 words Sinead gets 75% right. How many does she get wrong? **20 words wrong**

$$\frac{\cancel{80}^{20} \times 25}{\cancel{100}} = 20$$

A man wins £5,000 on the lottery. If he gives 25% to charity, how much does he keep for himself? **£3,750**

$$\frac{5,000 \times 75}{100} = 3,750$$

A man has to drive 240 km to get home from a business trip. If he has driven 35% of the journey, how much further does he have to go? **156 km**

$$\frac{240 \times 65}{100} = 156$$

Cyril's house cost £96,000. James's house cost 10% less. How much did James's house cost? **£86,400**

$$\frac{96,000 \times 90}{100}$$
$$\begin{array}{r} 960 \\ \times 90 \\ \hline 86,400 \\ \hline 5 \end{array}$$

Since the percentages and numbers here are larger, revisit page 5. The most likely error will come with children finding the percentage of the wrong amount, e.g., in the second question they may find 55% of 300, when the answer requires 45%.

Reading from scales

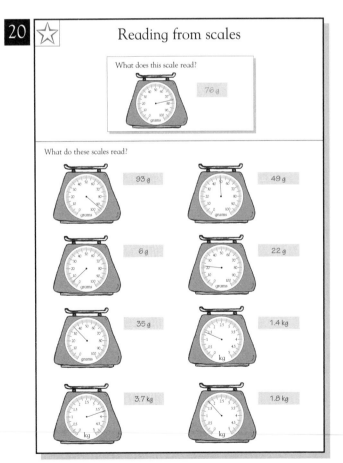

What does this scale read? **76 g**

What do these scales read?

93 g   **49 g**

6 g   **22 g**

35 g   **1.4 kg**

3.7 kg   **1.8 kg**

Reading the scales should be fairly straightforward. Use of a number line labelled in tenths would be a useful reinforcement.

Mean, median, and mode ⭐

Sian throws a dice 7 times. Here are her results:

4, 2, 1, 2, 4, 2, 6

What is the mean? $(4 + 2 + 1 + 2 + 4 + 2 + 6) ÷ 7 = 3$

What is the median?   Put the numbers in order of size and find the middle number, e.g., 1, 2, 2, 2, 4, 4, 6.

      The median is 2.

What is the mode?   The most common result, which is 2.

A school football team scores the following number of goals in their first 9 matches:
2, 2, 1, 3, 2, 1, 2, 4, 1

What is the mean score?   2

What is the median score?   2

Write down the mode for their results.   2

The ages of a local hockey team were:
17, 15, 16, 19, 17, 19, 22, 17, 18, 21, 17

What is the mean of their ages?   18

What is their median age?   17

Write down the mode for their ages.   17

The results of Susan's last 11 spelling tests were:
15, 12, 15, 17, 11, 16, 19, 11, 3, 11, 13

What is the mean of her scores?   13

What is her median score?   13

Write down the mode for her scores.   11

11 13 11 12 3

The work on this page teaches children the difference between the mean, the median, and the mode. The biggest problem they will have is remembering which is which. Encourage them to develop a system that works for them.

⭐ Area of compound shapes

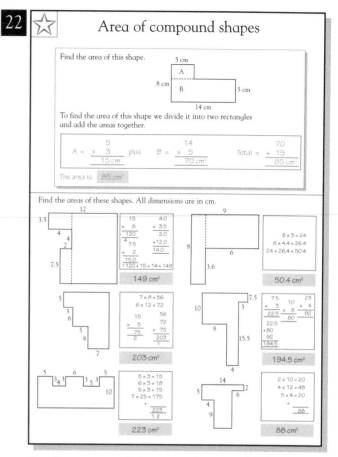

Find the area of this shape.

To find the area of this shape we divide it into two rectangles and add the areas together.

$$A = \begin{array}{r} 5 \\ \times\ 3 \\ \hline 15\ cm^2 \end{array} \quad plus \quad B = \begin{array}{r} 14 \\ \times\ 5 \\ \hline 70\ cm^2 \end{array} \quad Total = \begin{array}{r} 70 \\ +\ 15 \\ \hline 85\ cm^2 \end{array}$$

The area is   85 cm²

Find the areas of these shapes. All dimensions are in cm.

149 cm²

50.4 cm²

203 cm²

194.5 cm²

223 cm²

88 cm²

On this page and the next, the most likely difficulties will come in deciding how to split the shapes. If necessary, give assistance in finding a way of splitting the shape so that children get the dimensions necessary to do the calculation.

Area of compound shapes ⭐

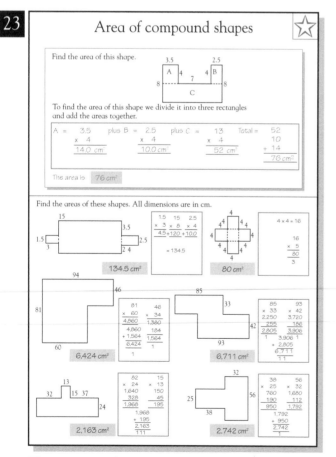

Find the area of this shape.

To find the area of this shape we divide it into three rectangles and add the areas together.

$$A = \begin{array}{r} 3.5 \\ \times\ 4 \\ \hline 14.0\ cm^2 \end{array} \ plus\ B = \begin{array}{r} 2.5 \\ \times\ 4 \\ \hline 10.0\ cm^2 \end{array} \ plus\ C = \begin{array}{r} 13 \\ \times\ 4 \\ \hline 52\ cm^2 \end{array} \ Total = \begin{array}{r} 52 \\ 10 \\ +\ 14 \\ \hline 76\ cm^2 \end{array}$$

The area is   76 cm²

Find the areas of these shapes. All dimensions are in cm.

134.5 cm²

80 cm²

6,424 cm²

6,711 cm²

2,163 cm²

2,742 cm²

This page reinforces practice in finding the area of compound shapes. As there are several ways of dividing shapes, children should use whichever they feel comfortable with.

⭐ Surface area of cuboids

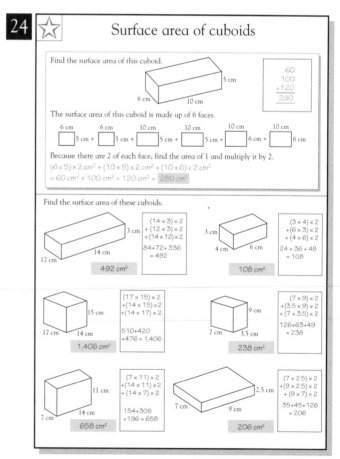

Find the surface area of this cuboid.

$$\begin{array}{r} 60 \\ 100 \\ +120 \\ \hline 280 \end{array}$$

The surface area of this cuboid is made up of 6 faces.

Because there are 2 of each face, find the area of 1 and multiply it by 2.

$(6 \times 5) \times 2\ cm^2 + (10 \times 5) \times 2\ cm^2 + (10 \times 6) \times 2\ cm^2$
$= 60\ cm^2 + 100\ cm^2 + 120\ cm^2 = 280\ cm^2$

Find the surface area of these cuboids.

$(14 \times 3) \times 2$
$+ (12 \times 3) \times 2$
$+ (14 \times 12) \times 2$
$84 + 72 + 336$
$= 492$ 492 cm²

$(3 \times 4) \times 2$
$+ (6 \times 3) \times 2$
$+ (4 \times 6) \times 2$
$24 + 36 + 48$
$= 108$ 108 cm²

$(17 \times 15) \times 2$
$+ (14 \times 15) \times 2$
$+ (14 \times 17) \times 2$
$510 + 420$
$+ 476 = 1,406$ 1,406 cm²

$(7 \times 9) \times 2$
$+ (3.5 \times 9) \times 2$
$+ (7 \times 3.5) \times 2$
$126 + 63 + 49$
$= 238$ 238 cm²

$(7 \times 11) \times 2$
$+ (14 \times 11) \times 2$
$+ (14 \times 7) \times 2$
$154 + 308$
$+ 196 = 658$ 658 cm²

$(7 \times 2.5) \times 2$
$+ (9 \times 2.5) \times 2$
$+ (9 \times 7) \times 2$
$35 + 45 + 126$
$= 206$ 206 cm²

This page takes the concept of finding the area of a rectangle a stage further, to finding the surface area of 3D shapes. Children may first do six areas and add them, or find each face area and multiply it by two. Practice with 3D shapes may be needed.

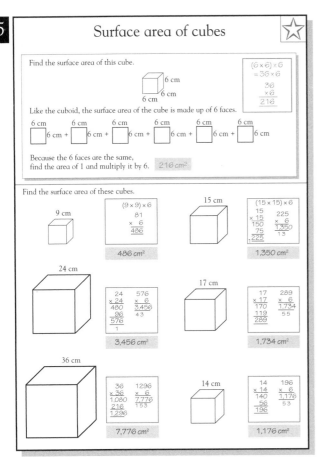

25 — Surface area of cubes

Find the surface area of this cube.

6 cm, 6 cm, 6 cm

(6 × 6) × 6
= 36 × 6

36
× 6
216

Like the cuboid, the surface area of the cube is made up of 6 faces.

6 cm | 6 cm + 6 cm | 6 cm + 6 cm | 6 cm + 6 cm | 6 cm + 6 cm | 6 cm + 6 cm | 6 cm

Because the 6 faces are the same, find the area of 1 and multiply it by 6.   216 cm²

Find the surface area of these cubes.

9 cm

(9 × 9) × 6
81
× 6
486

486 cm²

15 cm

(15 × 15) × 6
15
× 15
150
75
225

225
× 6
1,350
13

1,350 cm²

24 cm

24
× 24
480
96
576
1

576
× 6
3,456
43

3,456 cm²

17 cm

17
× 17
170
119
289

289
× 6
1,734
55

1,734 cm²

36 cm

36
× 36
1,080
216
1,296

1296
× 6
7,776
153

7,776 cm²

14 cm

14
× 14
140
56
196

196
× 6
1,176
53

1,176 cm²

If we find the surface area of one face we can multiply it by six to find the surface area of a cube. Children who are unsure may need to add the six areas together. Practical reinforcement using 3D shapes will help to clarify any confusion.

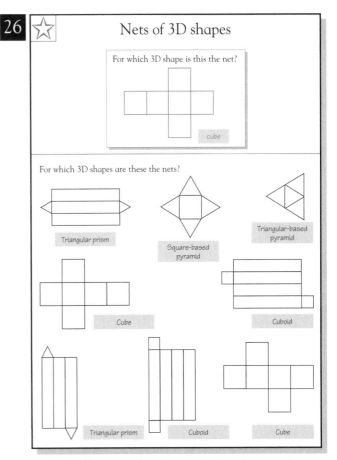

26 — Nets of 3D shapes

For which 3D shape is this the net?

cube

For which 3D shapes are these the nets?

Triangular prism

Square-based pyramid

Triangular-based pyramid

Cube

Cuboid

Triangular prism

Cuboid

Cube

Most children are familiar with the shapes of nets although they can find it more difficult to draw them. Some shapes, like the cube, have more than one net and it can be an interesting exercise to ask children to find as many different nets for the cube as they can.

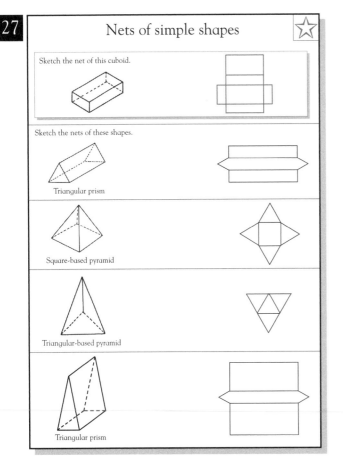

27 — Nets of simple shapes

Sketch the net of this cuboid.

Sketch the nets of these shapes.

Triangular prism

Square-based pyramid

Triangular-based pyramid

Triangular prism

If children experience problems on this page, it may be necessary to draw the nets on paper or card, and cut them out to see if they make the shape. If this is done, point out that nets do not require flaps.

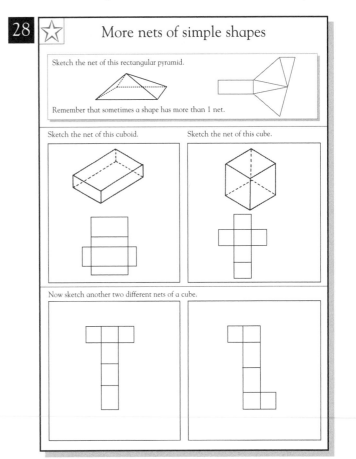

28 — More nets of simple shapes

Sketch the net of this rectangular pyramid.

Remember that sometimes a shape has more than 1 net.

Sketch the net of this cuboid.

Sketch the net of this cube.

Now sketch another two different nets of a cube.

These are the three likely nets of a cube that children may sketch; however, others are acceptable. If in doubt, sketch on squared paper and cut out to see if it will make a cube. If children found the previous page difficult, continue with the practical work.

Co-ordinates

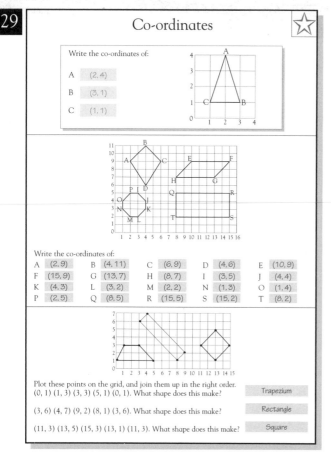

Write the co-ordinates of:

A (2, 4)

B (3, 1)

C (1, 1)

Write the co-ordinates of:

A	(2, 9)	B	(4, 11)	C	(6, 9)	D	(4, 6)	E	(10, 9)
F	(15, 9)	G	(13, 7)	H	(8, 7)	I	(3, 5)	J	(4, 4)
K	(4, 3)	L	(3, 2)	M	(2, 2)	N	(1, 3)	O	(1, 4)
P	(2, 5)	Q	(8, 5)	R	(15, 5)	S	(15, 2)	T	(8, 2)

Plot these points on the grid, and join them up in the right order.
(0, 1) (1, 3) (3, 3) (5, 1) (0, 1). What shape does this make? Trapezium

(3, 6) (4, 7) (9, 2) (8, 1) (3, 6). What shape does this make? Rectangle

(11, 3) (13, 5) (15, 3) (13, 1) (11, 3). What shape does this make? Square

Children should remember to read off the horizontal co-ordinate first. In the second section it is important that they join the co-ordinates in the order in which they are written to produce the shape.

Drawing angles including reflex

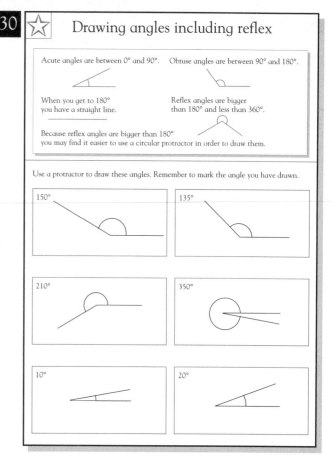

Acute angles are between 0° and 90°.   Obtuse angles are between 90° and 180°.

When you get to 180° you have a straight line.

Reflex angles are bigger than 180° and less than 360°.

Because reflex angles are bigger than 180° you may find it easier to use a circular protractor in order to draw them.

Use a protractor to draw these angles. Remember to mark the angle you have drawn.

150° 135°

210° 350°

10° 20°

To do the work on this page and the next, children require a 360° protractor. Check that they are reading the protractor from the right direction. Remind the children to mark the angles. This is important to avoid confusion when drawing reflex angles.

Drawing more angles including reflex

Draw these angles. Remember to mark the angle you have drawn.

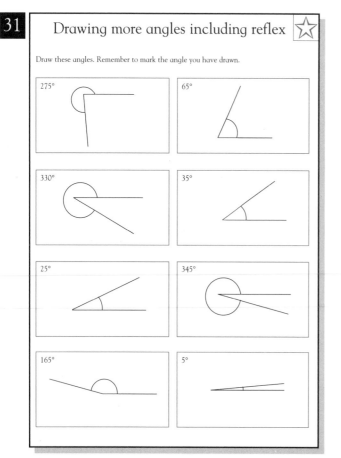

275° 65°

330° 35°

25° 345°

165° 5°

This page reinforces familiarity with angles and the use of protractors. On both this page and the previous one allow an error margin of plus or minus two degrees when checking the drawings.

Find the angle

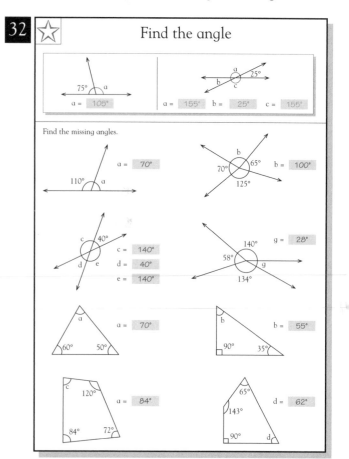

75° a   a = 105°

25° a = 155°   b = 25°   c = 155°

Find the missing angles.

110° a   a = 70°

70° 65° 125°   b = 100°

c 40° d e   c = 140°   d = 40°   e = 140°

140° 58° 134°   g = 28°

60° 50° a = 70°

90° 35° b = 55°

120° 84° 72°   a = 84°

65° 143° 90°   d = 62°

Finding unknown angles relies on the knowledge about angles adding up to 180° in a straight line and 360° at a point, and vertically opposite angles around a point being the same. Angles inside a triangle add up to 180° and those inside a quadrilateral add up to 360°.